The Yogini Poems:
Love and Life

The Yogini Poems :
Love and Life

Dr. Adyasha Das

BLACK EAGLE BOOKS
2020

BLACK EAGLE BOOKS

USA address:
7464 Wisdom Lane
Dublin, OH 43016

India address:
E/312, Trident Galaxy, Kalinga Nagar,
Bhubaneswar-751003, Odisha, India

E-mail: info@blackeaglebooks.org
Website: www.blackeaglebooks.org

First International Edition published by
Black Eagle Books, 2020

The Yogini Poems: Love and Life
by **Dr. Adyasha Das**

Copyright © **Dr. Adyasha Das**

All rights reserved. No part of this publication may be reproduced, stored in a retrieval system, or transmitted, in any form or by any means, electronic, mechanical, photocopying, recording or otherwise without the prior permission of the publisher.

Photo Credit: Adyasha Das

Cover and Interior Design: Ezy's Publication

ISBN- 978-1-64560-080-0 (Paperback)
Library of Congress Control Number: 2020940111

Printed in United States of America

To the Goddess in every woman

Preface

"A bird doesn't sing because it has an answer, it sings because it has a song."

— Maya Angelou

I can't recall when my tryst with poetry began; maybe when I wanted to give a glorious finish to a beautiful moment; or when I discovered the wonderful world of books. It came in with stray observations: summer showers, the moss-covered school wall, the lady at the bus-stop, undiagnosed aches, unexplained pleasures. Just when I was struck by my own thoughts, the musings of my own mind, poetry entered into me, almost like music.

Often I have been lazy, loving to laze in a bed of thoughts. Then, suddenly, like an unexpected downpour, the mysterious desire to write grasps me, and I put pen to paper. Writing is an excuse for me to delve deeply into the recesses of the mind, the labyrinth of alleyways between the conscious and the sub-conscious. Essentially, I write about matters which arouse my curiosity, the how's and why's of life events, situations etc. The art of creation is magical, the way a poem takes shape .But it gives me immense power, to watch my creation take form, often surprising even me. My words are an effort to immortalize thoughts, sentiments, people, and relationships in this transient world. I find myself always gathering luminous moments: the shimmer of golden snow on the Himalayan peaks, a pretty flower tucked away amidst wilderness, a stranger's smile, Neruda, Puri temple etc. I don't think I write poetry for any specific reason. I just write, as an intimate reflection of being me, as a kind of soul-speak, an impulse to reach out.

The literary ambience at home enthralled me. Great stalwarts of Indian & Odia literature, poets whom I held in awe, authors of all languages thronged our home. The discussion of thoughts and words, of stringing them together and adorning them with ornaments borrowed from all cultures invigorated me. The breeze of poetry wafted in me and I loved it. When I heard people recite poems, I swayed with the music of words, like the lilting melody of the music track of Dr. Zhivago. The library at home boasted books of all kinds, from all over the world. From science fiction, to fairy tales, world poetry to classics, modern drama to essays; my eyes feasted on all.

My first book of poems in English,"Nemesis" was published by The Writer's Workshop, Kolkata. "Anuccharita", my Odia book of poems followed soon after. "Brass Flowers", my third collection of poems, put together the wanderings of my mind. The journey continues with this new collection of poems which reflect my experiences with life and love and the sheer pleasure of creation. My family, friends and readers have all encouraged me to go ahead at all times.

This collection of poems is dedicated to the Yoginis I have met in course of my research and travel. From Hirapur, Ranipur Jharial, Khajuraho, Morena to Cambodia and Indonesia, I have met the Yogini's everywhere. The term Yogini includes a female practitioner of yoga, or ritual arts, a female being with magical powers, female deity and in the contemporary parlance, an empowered woman. A pronounced sense of sacredness and spirituality characterizes these women of the mystic Yogini cult. The Yogini temples stand as an embodiment of the venerated all powerful Divine female figure, the "Yogini". The enigma of these tantric goddesses intrigued me. In continuation of my books of research on the Yogini Cult, I wrote these poems as a tribute to the forgotten Yoginis. These poems are an attempt to write about the silence, light and space in the life and love meanderings of the Yogini.

The Yoginis have captivating appearances, both terrifying and mesmerizing and offer life-enhancing energies that bring about fertility, growth, longevity, abundance, material and spiritual well-being. Yoginis are wrathful and sensual, ferocious and seductive, furious and graceful. The poems reflect the longing of the Yoginis for companionship, undergoing significant transformations from a dominant status as a goddess, to a woman of the modern world. The relevance of the Chausathi Yoginis in contemporary times is celebrated in these poems.

Adyasha Das

CONTENTS

Chandika's Song	13
Chamber Music	15
For You, Shiva	17
Home	18
The Dark One	20
Hunger	22
Lead Me	23
Soul Bird	25
After You Left	26
The Music of Tantra	29
Brass Flowers	31
For You Caretaker	32
Narmada's Search	34
The Yogini's Ache	36
Truth Prevails	38
Carnal Flower	39
Come, Let's Age With Grace	42
My Words, Your Words	44
Pursuit of Truth	46
When Love Visits	48
Companion	49
The Real Life	51
Day in the Park	53
Mindscape	54
The Sacred Chant	56
Motherland	58
Rebirth	60

Remembrance	62
Quest for Whole	64
Yesterday Once More	65
Reflection of Life	67
Unfinished Dream	69
Words Come Easy	70
The Colour of Love	72
The Search	74
This World of Ours	76
The Change	78
Thoughts of Sky	79
A New Beginning	81
A Book-shelf Called Life	82
Prayer	84
You Have Got to Share	85
Vacation With Love	86
Comma	88
Cosmic Dance	89
Muse	91
River of Life	93
Tantric Nemesis	94
The Goddess Woman	96
The Yogini's Confession	98

Chandika's Song

I am Chandika,
The Yogini
The wind of bygone eras, the fire of the future
Alone, in this deserted temple
I see the sea flowing in the sky
And the sky submerged in the recesses of the sea.
The sea-gulls of my youth spiral up to the clouds
As my age takes a stroll on the waves of a timeless sea.
The Gods of the sea and sky urge me on
The journey that has begun must end.
I am a flame of intense, ancient nostalgia
Of moments lived, and moments unlived
Masculine yet feminine, creator yet created.
The sunset will take me home, into the luxury of oblivion.
But before that,
Let me be the murmur of the sea.
The sigh of misunderstood legends and myths
Let me mourn for the war ravaged world
And wonder at the humanity of humble gestures
The sunset will take me home, I know.
But I have already died before
With all those who have died around the world
The final journey will just be going away for a long vacation.

Exotica Goddess Chandika, Chausathi Yogini Temple, Hirapur

Chamber Music

This ethereal walk inside, leaning on your love
Retracing my steps into my innermost chamber
The seething alcove deep in me
Where the soul-searching music blows along

An intense urge to remove my masks
Layer after habitual layer
How light I feel as they drop off
And I face you, bare to my very soul

The goodness falls off first, that lovely smile
The pleasant talk and loving concern
The image that the world admires
The storm of beauty and roses
All disappear as we walk inwards
Must I go on?

The road ahead will writhe in wilderness
Darkness and negativity of betrayal and defeat
The swamp of doubts that will suck you in
Shall we go on?

But I know I can't stop
I have to go on in this journey inward
You must know the dark pillars in me

The boiling cauldron of jealousy and intolerance
The volcano of subdued power
The symphony is unraveling all
This chamber music

Will you be there when the story has been told?
Can you survive the trial of truth
To see the flower strewn pasture at the other end
To repaint the mute shades with brightness
Will you dance with me to this eternal rhythm?

For you, Shiva

Shiva,
You inhabit me like a wreathe of sadness
Coiled all over me and deep inside
Ever since you left, countless aeons ago!

What am I now?
A stone statue, a cold corpse,
Lifeless, Soul-less.

Except you, Shiva
No-one knows of the life ember flickering in me,
Almost dead, in the throes of killing pain
Beneath the mute stony surface, the wind ravaged face
Beneath thousand covers of Time
I am alive, even now.

Will you not come again, Shiva?
And repaint me with your intense colours,
Perch me on the highest boughs of love
The waiting wearies me.
Come, we will enact our roles
Yet again.

Home

The books and scriptures
All proclaimed Love is ethereal
A heavenly sojourn
A union of the minds.

In our moments of togetherness
we talked about mind,
meeting of the minds,
mind over the body.

I'm home-less, since you deserted me
without shelter, in this forgotten temple.
Let me stay in you
Warm, secure.
In the wee hours of the night,
the sudden tremor that flashes through you,
the wet moments that cling to you
like water in a stream
grass-flowers in a meadow
let me be in you.

You are my home.
My entire earth.
To blossom wildly in your hills and gardens
Run madly in your open lanes

The brilliant red of the fire in you
The green earth on which you recline
the freedom to savour all this
Let me make my home in you.

The Dark One

You are the Dark One
The darkest of all
Fire streaming from your core

Why have you decided to reside in me?
My frail body,
My delicate mind,
Can they contain the force of the mighty one?

You are the Dark One
You resuscitate me
To witness the divine dance
In an instant I know
I am the chosen one!

Exquisite Narmada, Chausathi Yogini Temple, Hirapur

Hunger

Your eyes glow
With the incandescence
Of a mysterious hunger

A hunger that becomes
A mad gale
Tearing at my window
To deliver the message

Shall we meet by the river
And empty this hunger into its depths?
Or shall we make it the dense winter
Draping itself over the tree laden with cherries?

I am your invisible woman
Of the deepening darkness
I am the sweet-scented jasmine
Unfolding the petals of my life

Between darkness and dawn,
Sleep and dreams
Make me your eternal hunger

Lead Me

I am venturing into an unknown land
Alone
Led only by your breath
The quivering of your heart against mine
The warmth of your eyes
Translucent in the sunlight

I crave for you
Intensely
Insanely
Without knowing your length and breadth
Without having my questions answered
Bound to you in the cord of trust

You alone can discover
the endless possibilities of this body and soul
amazingly congruent to yours
Shield me from hurt with the shroud of your smile
Erase all hurt with the softness of your lips

Lead me into this unknown land
After all,
All we have to do is
Imagine!

Chausathi Yogini Temple, Morena

Soul Bird

Deep in your chest
Glows the golden shine
Of the razor sharp sun-rays

Deep in your heart reverberate
Sagas of battles fought
Tales of valour

This temple is devoid of memories
Except you, the air I breathe
You, the sky of the underworlds

Let me dwell as the bird of your soul
Flitting from flower to flower
On the way out of this world.

After You Left

Had to tell you so much yesterday
unending tales of untold symphony's
Of tender thoughts locked in the wrinkled hand of Time
Yet ever fresh
Of the very first time I met you
Your initial awkward words of love,
Endless, intimate conversations on rainy mornings,
Ecstatically indifferent to both propriety and puddles
Of getting to know you over the years
Re-discovering you in a spectrum of colours.
My secret ways of looking at you
Thousand tiffs to make up , long forgotten.
Somehow, I never could tell you all I had to
Of the endless horizons of our relationship,
Planning for tomorrows, weaving dreams
Promises of togetherness,
Reaching out and pulling you closer, (something I was too busy to do lately)
Somehow I just could not tell you
What a treasure trove of love I had in me.

And suddenly you left.
Forever , forever.
Your last farewell, from this earthly abode.
You left, without any call, message.

Never to return like always, after the day's work
Sharing contentment over a cup of tea
Never to recline in the chair, in your inimitable style
Your smile warming me across the room.
Never to come back to your house, your garden
Not even to me, dearest .

Tears, prayers, offerings, worship
I have tried everything
Over and over again.
I know
Despite all I do now
Despite my love for you
There is no homecoming for you again .

But through this haze of unreality
I am doing all that is done
For the peace of the departed soul.
Do not offer me sympathy.
One word, and I will become an
Ocean of tears.
From this unfathomable ocean of tears
Others will gauge the depth of my agony.

Leave me alone
To immerse myself in grief for my beloved,
In my own way, beyond rites and rituals
I will regain control of myself soon.
Soon I'll reason out the regret,
of half spoken thoughts, thoughtless mistakes.
Love, I couldn't do so much that I should have.
Why didn't I readily agree with you

Why didn't I spend more time with you
How did time slip away from our clasp
In few moments,
you,
your awesome personality,
Your laurels,
All merges into a throbbing memory.

Life goes on, and I have to.
Without you
Perhaps I will live, like always.
Busy with responsibilities
Defying today,
Regretting each yesterday.
I will read, eat, smile.
In your absence.
As though nothing has changed, because you are not there.
The flowers will bloom in your garden.
The void you created in me,
Will not be known to anyone,
Nothing will change for anyone,
And while everyday they live.
I'll be dying a little.
Each new day.

The Music of Tantra

A complete cosmos within this void
In which I yearn to mingle
In the depths of nothingness
To be supremely complete

Isn't this because of you?
The subtle change in space and time
In your intangible drift
You silently invade my mind
And I am changed forever.

I am engulfed in an ocean of forgetting
What has been and what will be
Only a wordless communion
In the fathomless depths

Mystic Trance

Brass Flowers

Call me by any name
Give me any role
Ask anything
I have surrendered myself
In blind devotion
To your love

White or yellow
Choose any colour
Your mood for the day
I will wear that
with sincerity

Body or mind
Thoughts or touch
Your choice for the night
I'll cloak myself in it
With complete liberty

Don't you realize
Whether you make me the
fresh flower in your garden
Or the passionate brass flowers
of the paperweight you hold
I am stamped for all times

I seek no way out
Only the one way street in.

For You Caretaker

This house that I have lived in, all my life
My dream come true tryst with its body
The colour of the skin covering it
A dash of green here, turquoise flashes there
Fresh air to move in its many lanes
Roses, azaleas, daises in wild disarray
My house, my creation, my very own.

This house, mute witness
To the living sparks of my ambition
The worlds of suffering I have slipped into
Fine layer's of dust burying my laurels
Rivers of vanity thundering in my veins
The misty afternoons of surrender to the only one.

A day will come when the paint will peel off
Trickle of raindrops will seep into the carpet
The garden untended, weeds plundering it's beauty
A day will come when I won't be well
No longer marvelling at the beauty of your toe-nails
Mad journeys into the depths of your soul
Dressed in the pain that will be only mine
I can only be with you in my dream
Unguarded, without make-up
So close you could count the wrinkles of my soul

As I look at the dregs of my life
I know it's the last storm
I will have to leave behind everything
This house of memories
My very precious words
In gold covered books
The symphonies of summer breeze
Old photographs, dog-eared poems,
Beautiful jewellery from the world over
But more important, the landmark dates
Birthdays, anniversaries,my daughters smiles
Unexplained tragedies, unexpected happiness
Millions of bushels of my life

I know I can only tell you
My caretaker in life
Will you not be so in death?
The caretaker of this house of my life
Under the mantel-piece where we spent passionate moments
Lies the key to everything that was my life
Do what you want with it
My last gift in this hour of reckoning.
In this final going away
With all my love
My caretaker
In life and death

Narmada's Search

Don't know when it all began
Like an unnamed drizzle
To torrential showers
This eternal quest for the ideal one
Like the flowers I love,
The colours I crave,
The artifacts I admire
The terrains I roam,
An ideal soul-mate
Endowed with all the beauty of the earth
In body and mind.

There were many I met in the dark alleys
In faraway landscapes
On hidden sea-shores
Traipsing incognito paths.
The connoisseur of beauty that I am,
They all beckoned me.
With beautiful bodies
Lithe, agile, curvaceous,
Cloying, wanton wants
Just the way I liked.
Never imagined the rich variety of shapes and sizes,
Colour and skin.
All mine, for the asking.

How many dips I took in those forbidden depths
How delicious the feel of bodies talking
Limbs intertwined, lips exploring
Many journeys to heaven they were.
And in the aftermath of it all,
A shared contentment.

They came and went
The memories of their bodies are now dim
In the warmth of new ones.
How easy it is to find them!

But why is the search unending?
Is it that I have found life-less bodies?
Without the mind?

A mind to stimulate me from within
To share the wonders of life
Talk about shining stars and sea
Fresh gusts of breeze
In the stifled indoors of life.

Beyond the gaily-wrapped packages of bodies
The primeval hunger of the flesh
A monotonous, routine matter.
And then, nothingness.
Tired of it now, this unending familiarization
With shapes and sizes.
Where will I find a mind
That will fit mine?

The Yogini's Ache

I stand here
Alone, abandoned
Amidst these colossal ruins.
As far back as I can see, I hurl my life backwards
To the distant brilliance of the past.
Stealthily I step across the unheard of silence of my companion
I entreat the trees to speak, the stone walls to murmur
The sentinels of my past to speak only what I can hear.
Around me is the great surviving world
My arrogant ecstasy a thing of the past
The moss of shock and fear blissfully creeping over me.
The sun of the past has taken back its love
My mind is trapped in this weary body of stone.
Take all from me
but my power to realize that you are gone.

Yogini Goddess from Tamil Nadu
Source : Internet

Truth Prevails

There is no denying the truth
I tried hard to resist
To restrain its arrival
To constrict its path
But it just meandered around
To reach me another way
Truth took me by rude surprise
And collided into me.

The shock ripped off the gateway to my heart
I can't let go now,
Can just let it all in
The despair and anguish
The emptiness engulfing me
There is no denying the truth
Just learning to live with it.

It is strange
Speaking to you in this new language
Of utter silence.
In this vast expanse of loneliness
Is the deepest   connection with you.
You come to me as eternal truth
In the blossoms of flowers
The changing seasons
You remain forever
My truth.

Carnal Flower

Make me your carnal flower
Forget the mind binding, intellectual discourses
Make me dissolve in the trail of your passion.

We have been lying within each other
In the labyrinth of our minds
Myriad meetings of our Id's
Tasting the constellations of passion
Unwinding in the inner landscapes
Languid summers and embers of winter
All in the mind
Melting, dissolving
In quiet sighs

Relinquish the lilacs with plastic smiles
Read the transparencies of my eyes
Decipher the luminous skin
Sprinkle the silk of your touch on me
Revel in the revealed me
Braid my turbulent emotions
Bend me, mould me
To trust you through veils of uncertainties

Count the quivers rippling in me
When, unannounced you whisper passion
Dip your fingers in honey and
Unearth the buried lanes in me
Tangled forests and mystic pools
Watch me dance in the immense luxury of your rhythm
A timeless rhythm for an unlimited time

Come
Live with me in my solitude
Breathe with me
Discover me among sweet imperfections
Ever your carnal flower

The Elusive Chausathi Yoginis, Chausathi Yogini Temple, Hirapur

Come, Let's Age With Grace

And suddenly age stopped by
Looked me in the eye
Sent me on a roller-coaster ride
On the other side of the hill.

The lustre dimmed,
The glow dulled
I came to accept the face
Not so unfamiliar
Staring at me in the mirror

Night after ageing night
I see the same moon
Fiery in the inky backdrop
Same, yet not very same
A look-alike of the moon I knew.

The wrinkles I gather
Are sagas of life's vast tracts
And as I look at them,
I relive forgotten nuggets of gold
Rainy afternoons, clasped hands.

Leave we must
Each loss prepares us
From a broken doll
To a beloved departed

But till then,
Let me love fiercely
The delicious dreaming
Has just begun.

My Words, Your Words

These words that I string together
Garlands of them
With the embers of many moods
Completely mine for this moment in time
Yet never mine
But passed on since eternity

Whose hands had held it once under the canopy of twinkling stars?
Or behind shuttered lattices of windows
Who had uttered them with exultation?
Or as a sigh of a summer craze
Or even in the despair of living the last moment?
Who did those nimble fingers belong to?
All gone, lost
Only their imprint on these words
Vivid impressions of their lives
Encapsulated in these words
The silence of one or the joy cascading from another
Uniting souls across generations

And some day
When I am gone
My words will be yours
Will reach out to unknown souls

My words about everything and nothing
The gifts of this earth, the flowers and fruits
Children growing up too fast
Ghosts of lovers and sworn enemies
Of the sun and rains of life
How soon life ended
Even before it started
My words will be yours
And life will go on.

Pursuit of Truth

Eternal truth
So many seekers, so many ways
Ascetics, mendicants, writers, poets
Scientists, astrologers, priests
All of them
In search of the truth.

Whose truth is it?
Yours or mine.
Is my truth yours and your truth the worlds?
Does truth age too?
Does it fall sick, and rise up again?
Does it have a life
And then meets its end?

No glaring timeless verdict for me
Shards of glass that pierce my heart
Life is passing us by
With measured steps
The hour-glass of time all restless
No moments to spare for this search for truth

Tell me lies that are like wine
The   mint-tinged breath of the wind
Erase the scars of imperfection
Resurrect me in your abandonment of truth
All that I am not, all that I could'nt be
Truth I know, sets you free
Gift me eternal bondage

What moves is Her, What moves not, is also Her
Source : Internet

When Love Visits

I am ready to show you my home
Interiors laced with rust
But exterior walls bright
Like the sun serenading
The darkness of the moon

It is late in the day
The dreaming is all done
Yet the sunrays seep in
Through the cracks
An April mirage in December

Don't falter at the door
Walk in with yellow daisies
To brighten the dullness in me
The flesh shriveled, eyes shrunk
There is still love in me

A spoonful of words
A slice of the night that falls like rain
The flavor of faded love
This simple fare I offer
When you visit my home today

Companion

Be my companion
My alter-ego
Just mine

If you try, you can reach me.
The surface is rough, the climb tough.
Can you walk down a bit
Reach up a bit
Part the cobwebs
Invade the many masks I have chosen
Beyond the labyrinth of complex tunnels
I exist
Try,
Just once.

The road leading to me
is an unending expanse
There's no starting-point
No point of end
You to me
An eternal quest
Search for me
Just once.

Come.
Just once.
Hold my hand
Lets race to the moon
Away from the world.
My companion.

The brave Katyayini, Chausathi Yogini Temple, Hirapur

The Real Life

Life goes on.
Despite battlefields and blood-shed
Riots and massacres
Terrorism and honour killings,
Despite all that is dark and dreary,
Life goes on.

Life flows by in our home
Through moody seasons,
The sets of crockery changing over time
With members coming and going
The nondescript shop at the street corner
The glistening Taj Mahal in scorching summer
The silent Buddha statues of Borobudur
The forgotten ruins of Angkor Wat
Nothing, no-one escapes the touch of life.

Yet nothingness comes.
Like a bolt of lightning.
Like it has happened since eternity
Innocent lives snuffed out for no reason
The emptiness of losing loved ones
The terrifying world around us
The helplessness of this very minute "I".

The stream of living goes on
We notice once again forgotten springs
The beauty of each dawn that makes living worthwhile
The birches that outlived harsh winters
We wipe the tears of tragedies
And smile at the truant butterflies
Like so many lives before us
So many yet to come.

Day In The Park

Far away from you, I lie here
My thoughts running a marathon to you.

Of the stars in my sky and the shy sun in yours
My lonely night and your pleasant companions
Of the good deed you are doing
And the good deed I must do

Why are all the colours with you?
emerald green, passionate blue
the pink of love, crimson desire
When my world is covered with
A solitary sheet of darkness?

I see you walking amidst the grass
The wild profusion of flowers
Sharing your sparkling ideas
With your pleasant companions.

Next time, we must synchronize
our meetings with friends.
We must meet our separate friends
In our separate lives
At the same time.

Isn't it unfair?
In my longest miss-you moments
You have the shortest thoughts of me?

Mindscape

This mind.
This mind of yours, mind of mine.
A ceaseless wonder.
Now desert, now spring.

Just when I have walked all around it, felt the length and breadth
Just when I get comfortable in my abode
The furtive interplay of thoughts,
A new space opens up.

A by-lane I had never wandered down before.
Enticing in its summer light.
Attractive in its newness.
Yet, again the road constricts.
Suddenly closes in on me.
From all sides.
Claustrophobic blindness.
No space even to think of death.
Comfortable death.

Then the placid calm of the mind.
All quiet, even silence.
I can sleep on its surface
And weave a garland of thoughts.
Yet, again an abyss.

Slipping helplessly into its vortex
Spiraling down an unending , desolate space
Legends, myths, days, nights,
All rolled together.

This mind of ours,
Weaving towering structures
Demolishing cities and towns
A constant meandering of thoughts
Aching anguish, an abandoned romance
Unbuttoned leisure, tired tenderness
In the ultimate reckoning
All vanish
Into the space of mind.

The Sacred Chant

How can I not be in exile when you are on a holiday?
Exiled from the fireworks of life you bring
Caught between the time that has been,
The time that will be
All topsy turvy within me
While the world flows by normally

Everything's inevitable
Your vacation, meeting monarch butterflies
Becoming them, living your dreams
Then coming back to me
Oh, the pain in this going and coming
The misty downpour of sadness that is July

The sky around you, the stars you gaze at
The golden sand around your feet
The flirtatious moon, caressing your cheeks
All drive me crazy, green with jealousy
I remain your captive porcelain vase
A paper rose in the house we built

What will I do with all these?
Miss-you-moments you   gifted me.
Thread a garland for our together times
Or offer it in a temple as an amulet against threats?
Know my pain, feel my agony
Crashing over me in these hours of being alone.

Come, warm memories
Fill me up, every lonely inch of me
Be blossoms in the trees lining my backyard
The bird cooing the tune of better times soon!

The hypaethral Chausathi Yogini temple

Motherland

The sun never promised freedom.
But it is imprisoned amidst a web of clouds.
Bound by its vow,
The moon is crucified among the tentacles of branches.
But I had given my word
And so I am a prisoner.
I had promised to fight for my country's freedom
This confinement,
This dark cell,
How can it be a prison?
This deep night and its deeper sleep
Is eternal freedom.
I had promised to fight with my life
To free the sun
Release the moon.

In this solitude of the night
The stillness of my mind
Like words yearning to belong to a song
The song of freedom
But all are asleep
Entranced in an innocent stupor
Spellbound in the lullaby of friendship

The dawn will be cloudy today
They will shut out the sunlight
With a dark mask
And will escort me
To freedom
To merge in the light all around.

Before I don the black mask
Set aside for me
I wish to see you once,
With my entire vision
In your eyes I will see my motherland
Rivers, land, lanes, by-lanes
For the very last time.
My motherland will be mirrored
In the tears clouding your eyes.

I had promised you
Never to give up my life
But to gift it to my motherland.
Don't stop me.
I have given my word to love
My motherland and you
In life and death.
The question is only
At this very last hour
Whether you both remember me or not?

Rebirth

This time round,
The spring in my hometown
Came with a colour all its own
The world shrouded with just one grey canopy,
No barriers of distance, language or race
The universal canopy of fear
An unexplained, undiagnosed fear

In this utter helplessness, I have lived your life
And you are reliving my apprehensions
From the empty piazzas of Italy
To deserted Chinese pagodas
The silent temples of India, deserted roads of New York
Intimately connected in this distancing from each other.

A look back at the moments of glory
Of a world happy and gay
A global village of connections and networking
Now, only the saga of grief, anxiety all around
The finality of death, in numbers abound
All equal in the queue for death

Pour the balm of medication on tired minds
The belief of an ardent prayer for this world home of ours
Give us the green of forests, the smiles of innocent faces

The wealth of health, a longing of the soul
For we have trespassed, endure we must
Instil in us undying faith

These moments will be history,
This present will be past
The invisible enemy will retract its path
This too shall pass.
This too shall pass.

Remembrance

When will winter come?
Amidst the snowflakes, the blossom of spring will touch me
Here, there, everywhere.
And like all your winter garments
The light blue cashmere shawl with intricate embroidery
The chocolate – brown coat you love so much
Cots-wool clothes, suits, mufflers, gloves
You will suddenly remember me
Your precious me

With tremendous care, you'll dust off
Layers of mundane today's and tomorrows
You will spread me out in the tender sunlight
That the musty unused smell subdues.
The slow warmth of the iron melting the
Freezing clots of my mind.
I will revel in the anticipation, that
You do remember.
And one cold evening, your eyes are riveted on me
Your fingers tentatively play on my lonely mind,
I am choked with tears of all emotions
When suddenly you move on,
Choose something else to wear
Fold me, wrap me up with globules of naphthalene and care
And put me back on the shelf

With love, care and immense concern
I am too precious even for an occasional wear

Winter smilingly enters me
And I lie on the shelf
Willing you, for once
To stop caring
And uncaringly drape me, throw me, hold me tight
All over you

Quest for Whole

Why do you want me in parts only?
Few misty mornings, stolen moments
This and that of me, bits and pieces
Like the summer sky returning each year
No matter how sought after, how much craved for
Destined to come just once a year.

Who is your chosen Yogini this summer?
Who else is the rain in your skies
Life-giving , nourishing , refreshing rain?
A habit fostered for years
A connection not to be forgotten
A duty called commitment

Just for once
Discover the rain in me
The rainbow-hued sky, a frenzy of colours
Diamond drizzles to cleanse you
Of a past that has long been over
Maybe then, you will want me in rains too
After the sheen of summer
And we can think of a winter together.

Yesterday Once More

It was destined to be like this
Your love for me, mine for you
From this defined world of ours
To the undefined frontiers

To have loved you in the touchable boundaries
Of your beautiful eyes, your smooth face
And to continue that love in the sudden disappearance
To love fiercely in the grip of searing loss

The aching hurt of unkept promises, unsaid words
The love of shared gazes across the table
The loving remains as always,
Between two worlds, light and shade

Come back yesterday,
Just once, you need not stay.

Tantra Flower
Source : Internet

Reflection of Life

Who are you, painter?
Creator of this breathtaking piece
A cosmos in itself
Reflection of life

The hills and valleys
The hues of the leaves
The cloud's royal reflection
Life's mosaic

Listen to the whispering woods
The language of passion
The coolness of the water
assuaging warm yearnings

Green robes of youth
Cascades of waves for the adventurous
The grey of wisdom
Colours dreams are made of

Painter, I have lost my eloquence
Bereft of any thoughts
As I look at your creation
Only unfathomable tranquility

For all the sins I have committed
I must seek salvation
No holy chants or penance
Only to gaze at your masterpiece, painter.
To unravel the mysteries of life.
By looking at the reflection of life!

Unfinished Dream

Time crawls past
Winter readies for departure
Time betrayed me
And took away my treasure

The tight hand-clasp when we clung to each other
The promise of spending all time together
It remains true, we are inexplicably bound
Your presence fills the air, this truth I have found.

You are the light
The radiance of the dawn
Love's unwavering flame
In a heart that is torn.

Words Come Easy

Why do you want me to be tempered in silence
When I wish to decorate you with precious words?
My tongue of gold
To polish these words till they glow ruby

Words for your many moods
The glow of your scrubbed skin, cleansing the tiredness of time
Hidden rivers in which you search for a reflection
Your boats of friendship under strange constellations
The distant closeness of the haven called home

Words for your shimmering nights in flower-scented pastures
Weekdays freckled with duties and obligations
Riotous springs, colourful flowers
Planned vacations, unplanned dreams

They are all over me, don't you see?
These words.
In my music, seasons, moments,
The desire that is irrevocable.

They people my dreams, meet me in streets
Transform my days to years, youth to middle age
Undisguised, unconcealed, I can't hide from them

As I sleep in the soft bed they have made for me
I long to touch you intimately with them
To take away your mortal burdens, spice your mind.

Come.
The feast is for you.
You.
The molten gold of my tongue

The Colour of Love

Who would take care of me the way you do?
Who would listen to the symphony crafted in my mind?
With tender aches,
Aching desires of needs
Needed or not?
How easily the magic of your touch
Lifts my ordinary life to dizzy heights?

At times you whisk me off,
On a chariot of clouds,
to a faraway land of stars.

On wintry nights, you envelope me
in a blanket of desire.
Laugh like carefree daisies
in my barren garden
The whiff of breeze
Playing truant in the forgotten by-lanes of my memory.

I am liquid wax
To be reborn, re-crafted
In your mould
I will light up with a new sheen
Burning bright in the suffering
You have envisioned for me
The crisscross of directionless roads in me
Level them with you relentless arrogance.
The floods of misunderstanding on my river banks
Build a bridge with your compassion
Light my path on this dreamy, dreary road
Paint my eyes with only one colour,
The colour of love.

Bagan Sand Painting

The Search

Every moment in life
Every turquoise blue moment
Is a moment of choice.

Do you see me?
My devoted mirror-images
Leafless in this sombre hour
To be decked with colours tomorrow

This body I call mine
This elusive soul
This body and soul
Laden with countless possibilities
Despite the barren exterior
A fertile mind creating several alter-egos.

There's only one, though
Which is me.
Beyond the superficial layers
Beneath the coating of civilization
Above gnarled rules and proscriptions
Only one me
With a rare congruence of the chooser and the chosen
A primordial connection.

But which of these is me?
They are all me
Fleeting possibilities
Transient time
Soon it will be dawn
Can I find my true me
In this life
On this turquoise, blue night?

This World of Ours

This world of ours, transient, touch and go
A bubble in the air, hovering in the shade of many worlds
Pulling me out of a thoughtless abyss
Only to shove me back there again.

Writhing amidst these lonely waves
I seek the asylum of our world
In this madness of mine
I forget the reality, the real world, the one we live in

This world of ours, just a wax image
Of blossoms, fruits and love
Almost like it should be
But never to be.

Mahamaya, the presiding deity, Chausathi Yogini Temple, Hirapur

The Change

How strange this life
A game of lost and found
So many faces, the most loving
Warm moments of forbidden intimacy
Dog-eared secrets, stray summer madness
In an instant lose their significance
And merge with the ordinary
Lifeless, colourless, they lie untended
Who designs this change?
An eternally blamed destiny?
A mute God?
Or a nude mind?
Flitting like a bird
From the breath of the past
To a vulnerable present
To the desire of the future.
A life coloured with change.

Thoughts of Sky

My constant companion, you azure sky
Teaching me the mantra of life
A parikrama of the journey on earth
Through endless trials and tribulations
To merge with the dust in the end
With you as my shroud forever.

The crystalline clear morning,
adorned with latticed gold rays
Your unforgiving visage in the heat of the noon
Tenderness of honeysuckle on dusky evenings
Starlit nights and asphalt darkness at times
All your moods, just like life

Rain comes some days and touches us both
Cleansing the soul to look at you anew
Something which I forget to do
In the hustle and bustle of life
Though you unfailingly remain my alter-ego

When all is pain and misery, death and destruction
You remain royally aloof
Gentleness dripping in sheets of blue
Hope in the fiery orange of dawn
Muti-coloured mosaic of rainbows
The blush of rose in twilight

At some point in time as you change your robes
I write poetry borrowing your lustre
Of incorruptible desires, translucent minds
Every day the desire to rise up to you
To find the right road in the labyrinth of life.

A New Beginning

A minute, an hour, a lifetime of memories
Words, smiles, jewels of togetherness
There are no words in this moment of parting
For it is but your new beginning
You are the sound of birds, of rain,
The music of almost everything
The touch of lilies in many-hued bloom
The vision of the pale pink dawn

Across the distance, I know you care
You are with me, you always were.

A Bookshelf Called Life

A bookshelf called life
Filled with books
Age-old treasures, recent editions
Books of reference on life.

Forgotten books of carefree childhood
Intense poems of growing up
Happy sonnets of joyful moments
Heartbreaking songs of sorrow

Books on all that I wanted to be
about almost reaching the finish line
Success and failure, war and peace
Treachery and malice
Of all that the world is.
Of all that the world could be.

Books on faith
On someone called God
A terrifying reality
Mostly forgotten when the going is good
Desperately needed in the darkest hour.

And then there is a shelf on you
Books on your many moods and shades

At times sheer jubilation
Choosing and being chosen
Narratives on the "id" you camouflage
the labyrinths of the mind
but mostly, surely
Books on loving
A universality transcending inner, outer borders.

In the bookshelf of my life
The only shelf that is incomplete
Keeps adding new editions and reprints
Brand new books
Different from yesterday
Newer than today, You!

Prayer

My prayer
Private, most confidential
Desperate, anguished
An ardent entreaty
A seductive persuasion
To resurrect my will, want, desire
Only mine, just mine.

My prayer, amidst everyday chores
As afternoon glides into dusk
In the exalted portals of the temple
Between the kitchen and the back-yard
Anywhere, everywhere
Resuscitates me
Makes my wishes come true.
How convenient that you are stone-silent
Destined never to speak
Giving me, and all others
The illusion of agreement
In exchange for a coconut, clothes and
One bright wick of a lamp called life?

You Have Got to Share

This mind of mine is spent in bits and pieces
Everywhere
One just has to share this very own self
Like planting the seeds of life
Without a reckoning of seasons
Even then,
Somewhere the weather becomes ruthless
Destroying the crop
Or starving the rice fields.

If only
I could have shared myself
Like the wind
Become the rain dancing all over the Earth
If only I could have smiled like the blossoming flowers
Even while looking at my enemies,
If only I could have filled with fragrance their brutality.

I would have lent the sun's warmth to the dry logs
The calming touch of the moon
Wherever needed
Would have risen on both sides of the horizon
In the hearts of friends and enemies alike
Like the tree standing tall in scorching heat
If only I could have gifted life-saving shade to my killer

If only,
If only I could have given away all my achievements
To this world
Unasked.

Vacation with Love

I am covered with you
Lot of me, most of me
You took long back.

Never believed that time was irreversible
Till you invaded my cage
And changed all seasons
To eternal spring

My small-town fame
Attempts at creating
Symphonies from nourishing pain
To create worlds with words
To lead a life of acceptance
Nothing can keep me from
Playing with this breeze I am.

Till you return
Let me cover myself with you
The multi-coloured quilt of delight
Let Bach create music
Dostoevsky meddle with words
I am on vacation with love

The Shy Yogini, Chausathi Yogini Temple, Hirapur

Comma

I wonder about you
This and that of you
The elusive quick-silver streaks in you
There, yet not there

I am mesmerised by
The entranced quietude in you
Your calmness.
Almost peace,
Almost tranquillity

Don't call me
To openness
To light
How do I tell you that
From the epic poem you have composed for me
A "comma" alone
Can give me
A cosmos of happiness.

Cosmic Dance

The alchemy of love blurs the borders
Mysteries wed fantasies
In this divine dance
Looking up at the stars
From this hypaethral temple
We climb the sublime peak

We have reached the slippery space at the top
With the Sun and Moon as the witnesses
Saffron is the colour of my passion
Luxuriant , the garden blooming in me
The timelessness of a deep communion

I wear you in an infinite embrace
In complete surrender to eternity
I see the source of all creation
The Cosmic dance of eternity

Chausathi Yogini temple, Ranipur Jharial

Muse

Who painted the ocean in the sky,
Nimble fingers camouflaging the waves as clouds
Tumultuous and terrifying one moment
Soothing shadows the next?

Who taught the birds to fly high
Spiralling up and down in an intricate dance
Racing against the goals they set?

Who created the tapestry of love
Intertwined minds and bodies
The miracle of the night's drizzle of passion
A profusion of wild dreams
Music of moans to ecstatic sighs
Of surrendering, sharing oneness?

Creator, are you my Muse?
Handing me words and thoughts of your choice,
Colouring my eyes with your vision
To admire your breathtaking handiwork
Bound to you in the primordial bond?

Or am I creating you?
Erasing a bit here, adding some more there
Putting you on a pedestal
Then banishing you into a long exile?

Your sea, birds, mountains,
Human bodies and beautiful minds
All people me
Walk in me, in the corridors of my house

When sad, your sea turns pensive
When happy, the cuckoo sings.
What is it then?
This equation between us?
Are you a brilliant reflection of all that I am,
My God, my very own?
Or do you craft me the way you please?

Hold my hand, Creator.
Don't you see we have thousand things to create?
Before Time vanquishes me
Vagueness colours me
Let us create the world
Create each other
A final time.

River of Life

Oh, for a whiff of cool breeze on a sultry afternoon
The beauty of golden sun-rays in darkness
In this asphalt night, the craving for a shooting star
The smiling crescent of the moon.

Like the breeze
Lost in it on an unhurried morning
A chance meeting with it on a dusky evening
In a single moment
To gather up all my love
And offer this entire night.

Like the light
A quivering rainbow with its touch
Wearing the cool garb of the moon
The harsh glare of the afternoon.

In the oasis of life,
In the pyramid of half-built desires
I
Like the light
Like the breeze
In the river of life

Tantric Nemesis

Coffee-brown eyes
Sepia satin sensuality
Their aching beauty.

Nenuphar's language in them
In the mirror-world of tears
Words in a transcendental language of the senses.

A shaded colour
A lighted line
Unlooked for symmetries.

Whispering new gazes,
Barely heard, barely glimpsed
Labyrinthal, between earth and sky

A look back relives the hurt
Calxes of subtracted conversations
A look ahead, where, where?

A death wish
How could things have gone otherwise?
Nemesis

Chausathi Yogini Ghat, Varanasi

The Goddess Woman

I am the Goddess Woman
As I make my transition
From the fiery Yogini to the modern woman
I dare to rewrite history
I have loved Shiva too fondly
To be fearful of rejection

He taught me to see
The mantra underlying each sin
The dark roses of forbidden love
The tangled forests of ancient knowledge
The crumbling Time and space

Take away this body of stone
The head-dress and the weapons
Help me step down from this alcove
I am the woman of today
The goddess of my world

Creator of my new identity
I symbolize my ancestral past
Shape-less, formless
I mingle with the present
I am the woman of today
The goddess of my world

The Omniscient One
N.G.K. Nair Kocheril

The Yogini's Confession

When did I first realize I was different
That I saw differently
Felt differently
My pleasures had rare origins
My sorrows unique sources
The world wound around me
Yet I remained alone!

This mystery of me
Of the sun's gold hues
As I age and change
Is destined to be alone.
Traditions reject me
Modernism mocks at me
A dark image
A stained glass.

Yet the bells still toll in me
Music fills this different me
I am everything
A fish, amber-coloured glass beads,, the river, this evening.
Chipped and bent, defeated and abandoned
I am also nothing.
Between these two extremes
I oscillate
A rhythmic swing of mind
Called life.

What is, is Her

Books by Dr. Adyasha Das

- **The Chausathi Yoginis of Hirapur: from Tantra to Tourism** (ISBN-978-1-64560-012-1) - Non-fiction / English - Black Eagle Books
- **The Journey Starts Here: Global Management And Tourism Trends** (ISBN- 978-1-64560-063-3) - Non-fiction / English - Black Eagle Books
- **Bhitaraku Rasta** (ISBN - 978-1-64560-065-7)- Short Story / Odia - Black Eagle Books
- **Transgression and Other Stories** (ISBN- 978-1-64560-075-6)- Edited Short Story of Dr. Pratibha Ray / English - Black Eagle Books
- **Selected Poems of Emily Dickinson** (ISBN-978-1-64560-071-8) Edited Poems of Emily Dickinson / English - Black Eagle Books
- **Nemesis** - Poetry/English - Writer's Workshop
- **Anuccharita** - Poetry/ Odia - Adya Prakashani
- **Brass Flowers** - Poetry/English - Bird Nest
- **A bridge called culture: a sojourn of German landscapes** - Travelogue / English - Bird Nest
- **Changing values and Leadership Styles- a case study of Indian Police-** Non-fiction / English - Gyanajuga Publication

www.ingramcontent.com/pod-product-compliance
Lightning Source LLC
Chambersburg PA
CBHW042128100526
44587CB00026B/4220